MW00948818

Universe is Listening

This Journal Belongs To

_____

_____

Gratitude Journal

"**YOU** yourself
as much as

 **ANYBODY**

in the entire **UNIVERSE**

DESERVE

your **LOVE & AFFECTION**

– Gautama The Lord Buddha

Message from Author

When you want to get ahead in life, don't overthink, doubt yourself or your self-worth. Focus on only what you want. Visualize it, feel it and start living it every day as you have it already. We are all writing our own destiny in our own timeline. It is what we think about ourselves, that matters the most in life. So, manifest your thoughts confidently, positively, and vividly. It's only you that holds the key to endless possibilities.

— Asema Hassan

Date : 01 / 01 / 2022   **SAMPLE**   Feeling: ☹ ☹ ☺ ☺ ☺ ✓

Today, I am grateful for living in beautiful home, having warm meals,
having a loveable family and friends, clean water, a successful job, beautiful body,
an abundance of money, healthy lifestyle, freedom to live, travel & eat.
I am thankful for having the best lifepartner on my side, having healthy and smart
kids. I am grateful for what my life has become and what it offers everyday. :)

Positive Affirmations

I am a confident, beautiful, and a successful person.
I am loveable, energetic, healthy, and full of joy.
I am creating life of passion and purpose.
I am living a dream life with abudance of money and happiness everyday.
I am wealthy and successful in every aspect of my life.

Date : 02 / 01 / 2022   Feeling: ☹ ☹ ☺ ✓ ☺

Today, I am grateful for waking up alive, healthy and energetic.
going out for walk in sunny weather and feeling the sunshine on my skin.
I am thankful for people who loves me and cherish every momnent of our life together.
I am glad to have parents and friends who always stood by me & support my ideas.
I am grateful for getting promoted at work and getting the salary raise.

Positive Affirmations

I am healthy, beautiful, confident and successful person.
I am successful in every aspect of life and my business is growing everyday.
I trust Universe and ready to receive all it has to offer to me.
I am creating life of my dreams and very happy about what I have become.
I have health, love and money in abundance.

"Happiness is when what you think, what you say, and what you do are in harmony."

— Mahatma Gandhi

Date : ..../..................../...................   Feeling: 😖 😣 😐 😊 😄 − ▬▬▬▬▬ +

Today, I am grateful for _____

_____

_____

_____

_____

Positive Affirmations

I am _____

_____

_____

_____

_____

66   Favorite Quote   **99**

Date : ..../..................../...................   Feeling: 😖 😣 😐 😊 😄 − ▬▬▬▬▬ +

Today, I am grateful for _____

_____

_____

_____

_____

Positive Affirmations

I am _____

_____

_____

_____

_____

Date : ..../..................../.................   Feeling: 😣 😟 😐 😑 😊

Today, I am grateful for _____

_____

_____

_____

_____

Positive Affirmations

I am _____

_____

_____

_____

_____

❝   Favorite Quote   ❞

Date : ..../..................../.................   Feeling: 😣 😟 😐 😑 😊

Today, I am grateful for _____

_____

_____

_____

_____

Positive Affirmations

I am _____

_____

_____

_____

_____

Date : ..../....................../................   Feeling: 😟😞😐😊😄

Today, I am grateful for _____

_____

_____

_____

_____

Positive Affirmations

I am _____

_____

_____

_____

_____

66   Favorite Quote   99

Date : ..../....................../................   Feeling: 😟😞😐😊😄

Today, I am grateful for _____

_____

_____

_____

_____

Positive Affirmations

I am _____

_____

_____

_____

_____

Date : ..../......................./................   Feeling: 😞 😟 😐 🙂 😄
                                                            _ ▬▬▬▬▬▬▬ +

Today, I am grateful for _____

_____

_____

_____

_____

                           Positive Affirmations

I am _____

_____

_____

_____

_____

66   Favorite Quote   99

Date : ..../......................./................   Feeling: 😞 😟 😐 😐 🙂
                                                            _ ▬▬▬▬▬▬▬ +

Today, I am grateful for _____

_____

_____

_____

_____

                           Positive Affirmations

I am _____

_____

_____

_____

_____

Date : ..../................./................

Feeling:

Today, I am grateful for _____

_____

_____

_____

_____

Positive Affirmations

I am _____

_____

_____

_____

_____

> ## Favorite Quote

Date : ..../................./................

Feeling:

Today, I am grateful for _____

_____

_____

_____

_____

Positive Affirmations

I am _____

_____

_____

_____

_____

Date : ....../.............../.............   Feeling: 😊😊😊😊😊

Today, I am grateful for _____

_____

_____

_____

_____

Positive Affirmations

I am _____

_____

_____

_____

_____

66   Favorite Quote   **99**

Date : ....../.............../.............   Feeling: 😞😐😐😐😊

Today, I am grateful for _____

_____

_____

_____

_____

Positive Affirmations

I am _____

_____

_____

_____

_____

Date : ..../................../................　　　　　　　Feeling: 😠 😐 😐 🙂 😊

Today, I am grateful for _____

_____

_____

_____

_____

Positive Affirmations

I am _____

_____

_____

_____

_____

❝　　　　　　　　Favorite Quote　　　　　　　　**❞**

Date : ..../................../................　　　　　　　Feeling: 😠 😐 😐 🙂 😊

Today, I am grateful for _____

_____

_____

_____

_____

Positive Affirmations

I am _____

_____

_____

_____

_____

Date : ..../................../.................   Feeling: 😟 😞 😐 😕 😊

Today, I am grateful for _____

_____

_____

_____

_____

Positive Affirmations

I am _____

_____

_____

_____

_____

66   Favorite Quote   99

Date : ..../................../.................   Feeling: 😟 😞 😐 😕 😊

Today, I am grateful for _____

_____

_____

_____

_____

Positive Affirmations

I am _____

_____

_____

_____

_____

Date : ..../................/................   Feeling: 😟 😕 😐 🙂 😊
                                                          − ‒‒‒‒‒‒‒‒‒‒ +

Today, I am grateful for _____

_____

_____

_____

_____

Positive Affirmations

I am _____

_____

_____

_____

_____

" Favorite Quote "

Date : ..../................/................   Feeling: 😟 😕 😐 🙂 😊
                                                          − ‒‒‒‒‒‒‒‒‒‒ +

Today, I am grateful for _____

_____

_____

_____

_____

Positive Affirmations

I am _____

_____

_____

_____

_____

Date : ..../................../................   Feeling: 😫 😕 😐 🙂 😄
                                                        _ ▬▬▬▬▬▬ +

Today, I am grateful for _____
_____
_____
_____
_____

                        Positive Affirmations
I am _____
_____
_____
_____
_____

❝   Favorite Quote   ❞

Date : ..../................../................   Feeling: 😫 😕 😐 🙂 😄
                                                        _ ▬▬▬▬▬▬ +

Today, I am grateful for _____
_____
_____
_____
_____

                        Positive Affirmations
I am _____
_____
_____
_____
_____

Date : ..../......../........   Feeling: 😞 😐 😐 🙂 😊

Today, I am grateful for _____

_____

_____

_____

_____

Positive Affirmations

I am _____

_____

_____

_____

_____

66   Favorite Quote   99

Date : ..../......../........   Feeling: 😞 😐 😐 🙂 😊

Today, I am grateful for _____

_____

_____

_____

_____

Positive Affirmations

I am _____

_____

_____

_____

_____

Date : ..../................../...................   Feeling: 😊 😊 😊 😊 😊
                                                                        –   +

Today, I am grateful for _____

_____

_____

_____

_____

                              Positive Affirmations
I am _____

_____

_____

_____

_____

66   Favorite Quote   **99**

Date : ..../................../...................   Feeling: 😊 😊 😊 😊 😊
                                                                        –   +

Today, I am grateful for _____

_____

_____

_____

_____

                              Positive Affirmations
I am _____

_____

_____

_____

_____

Date : ..../..................../..................   Feeling: 😊😐😊😊😊 – ———— +

Today, I am grateful for _____

_____

_____

_____

_____

Positive Affirmations

I am _____

_____

_____

_____

_____

66   Favorite Quote   99

Date : ..../..................../..................   Feeling: 😞😐😐😊😊 – ———— +

Today, I am grateful for _____

_____

_____

_____

_____

Positive Affirmations

I am _____

_____

_____

_____

_____

Date : ..../...................../...................

Feeling:

Today, I am grateful for _____

_____

_____

_____

_____

Positive Affirmations

I am _____

_____

_____

_____

_____

66 Favorite Quote 99

Date : ..../...................../...................

Feeling:

Today, I am grateful for _____

_____

_____

_____

_____

Positive Affirmations

I am _____

_____

_____

_____

_____

Date : ..../.............../................   Feeling: 😕 😣 😐 😑 😊

Today, I am grateful for _____

_____

_____

_____

_____

Positive Affirmations

I am _____

_____

_____

_____

_____

66   Favorite Quote   99

Date : ..../.............../................   Feeling: 😣 😐 😑 😊 😊

Today, I am grateful for _____

_____

_____

_____

_____

Positive Affirmations

I am _____

_____

_____

_____

_____

"We are shaped by our thoughts, we become what we think."

— Gautama The Lord Buddha

Date : ..../................../................ Feeling: 😞😐😐😊😄

Today, I am grateful for _____

_____

_____

_____

_____

Positive Affirmations

I am _____

_____

_____

_____

_____

66 Favorite Quote 99

Date : ..../................../................ Feeling: 😞😐😐😊😄

Today, I am grateful for _____

_____

_____

_____

_____

Positive Affirmations

I am _____

_____

_____

_____

_____

Date : ..../................../....................

Feeling: 😞 😐 😐 🙂 😊
– ▬▬▬▬ +

Today, I am grateful for _____

_____

_____

_____

_____

Positive Affirmations

I am _____

_____

_____

_____

_____

66   Favorite Quote   99

Date : ..../................../....................

Feeling: 😞 😐 😐 🙂 😊
– ▬▬▬▬ +

Today, I am grateful for _____

_____

_____

_____

_____

Positive Affirmations

I am _____

_____

_____

_____

_____

Date : ..../.................../................   Feeling: 😷😐😐😊😄

Today, I am grateful for _____

_____

_____

_____

_____

Positive Affirmations

I am _____

_____

_____

_____

_____

66   Favorite Quote   99

Date : ..../.................../................   Feeling: 😷😐😐😊😄

Today, I am grateful for _____

_____

_____

_____

_____

Positive Affirmations

I am _____

_____

_____

_____

_____

Date : ..../................../................   Feeling: 😡😣😐😊😄
— ▬▬▬▬ +

Today, I am grateful for _____

_____

_____

_____

_____

Positive Affirmations

I am _____

_____

_____

_____

_____

66   Favorite Quote   **99**

Date : ..../................../................   Feeling: 😡😣😐😊😄
— ▬▬▬▬ +

Today, I am grateful for _____

_____

_____

_____

_____

Positive Affirmations

I am _____

_____

_____

_____

_____

Date : ..../......./............   Feeling: 😣 😔 😐 😊 😄

Today, I am grateful for _____

_____

_____

_____

_____

Positive Affirmations

I am _____

_____

_____

_____

_____

" Favorite Quote **"**

Date : ..../......./............   Feeling: 😣 😔 😐 😊 😄

Today, I am grateful for _____

_____

_____

_____

_____

Positive Affirmations

I am _____

_____

_____

_____

_____

Date : ..../..................../....................   Feeling: 😟 😐 😐 😐 😊

Today, I am grateful for _____

_____

_____

_____

_____

Positive Affirmations

I am _____

_____

_____

_____

_____

66   Favorite Quote   99

Date : ..../..................../....................   Feeling: 😟 😐 😐 😐 😊

Today, I am grateful for _____

_____

_____

_____

_____

Positive Affirmations

I am _____

_____

_____

_____

_____

Date : ..../............../..............   Feeling: 😐😟😐😊😄

Today, I am grateful for _____

_____

_____

_____

_____

Positive Affirmations

I am _____

_____

_____

_____

_____

66   **Favorite Quote**   **99**

Date : ..../............../..............   Feeling: 😐😟😐😊😄

Today, I am grateful for _____

_____

_____

_____

_____

Positive Affirmations

I am _____

_____

_____

_____

_____

Date : ..../.................../..................   Feeling: 😐 😐 😐 😐 😐
                                                                   _ ▬▬▬▬▬ +

Today, I am grateful for _____

_____

_____

_____

_____

Positive Affirmations

I am _____

_____

_____

_____

_____

66   Favorite Quote   99

Date : ..../.................../..................   Feeling: 😐 😐 😐 😐 😐
                                                                   _ ▬▬▬▬▬ +

Today, I am grateful for _____

_____

_____

_____

_____

Positive Affirmations

I am _____

_____

_____

_____

_____

Date : ..../............../...............   Feeling: 😐😕😐😊😄

Today, I am grateful for _____

_____

_____

_____

_____

Positive Affirmations

I am _____

_____

_____

_____

_____

66   Favorite Quote   99

Date : ..../............../...............   Feeling: 😕😐😕😊😊

Today, I am grateful for _____

_____

_____

_____

_____

Positive Affirmations

I am _____

_____

_____

_____

_____

Date : ..../................./.................　　　　Feeling: 😊 😊 😊 😊 😊
　　　　　　　　　　　　　　　　　　　　　　　　　　－ ▬▬▬▬▬▬▬ ＋

Today, I am grateful for _____

_____

_____

_____

_____

Positive Affirmations

I am _____

_____

_____

_____

_____

66　　　　　　　Favorite Quote　　　　　　　**99**

Date : ..../................./.................　　　　Feeling: 😟 😐 😐 😊 😊
　　　　　　　　　　　　　　　　　　　　　　　　　　－ ▬▬▬▬▬▬▬ ＋

Today, I am grateful for _____

_____

_____

_____

_____

Positive Affirmations

I am _____

_____

_____

_____

_____

Date : ..../................../................   Feeling: 😠😕😐😊😄

Today, I am grateful for _____

_____

_____

_____

_____

Positive Affirmations

I am _____

_____

_____

_____

_____

66   Favorite Quote   99

Date : ..../................../................   Feeling: 😠😕😐😊😄

Today, I am grateful for _____

_____

_____

_____

_____

Positive Affirmations

I am _____

_____

_____

_____

_____

Date : ..../.................../...................   Feeling: 😊😊😊😊😊

Today, I am grateful for _____

_____

_____

_____

_____

Positive Affirmations

I am _____

_____

_____

_____

_____

66   Favorite Quote   **99**

Date : ..../.................../...................   Feeling: 😊😐😐😊😊

Today, I am grateful for _____

_____

_____

_____

_____

Positive Affirmations

I am _____

_____

_____

_____

_____

Date : ..../..................../..................   Feeling: 😠 😟 😐 🙂 😊

Today, I am grateful for _____

_____

_____

_____

_____

Positive Affirmations

I am _____

_____

_____

_____

_____

66   Favorite Quote   **99**

Date : ..../..................../..................   Feeling: 😠 😟 😐 🙂 😊

Today, I am grateful for _____

_____

_____

_____

_____

Positive Affirmations

I am _____

_____

_____

_____

_____

Date : ..../................../................

Feeling:

Today, I am grateful for _____

_____

_____

_____

_____

_____

Positive Affirmations

I am _____

_____

_____

_____

_____

66   Favorite Quote   99

Date : ..../................../................

Feeling:

Today, I am grateful for _____

_____

_____

_____

_____

_____

Positive Affirmations

I am _____

_____

_____

_____

_____

Date : ..../...................../..................   Feeling: 😟 😐 🙂 😊 😄

Today, I am grateful for _____

_____

_____

_____

_____

Positive Affirmations

I am _____

_____

_____

_____

_____

66   Favorite Quote   99

Date : ..../...................../..................   Feeling: 😟 😐 🙂 😊 😄

Today, I am grateful for _____

_____

_____

_____

_____

Positive Affirmations

I am _____

_____

_____

_____

_____

"Life is a balance of holding on and letting go."

— Rumi

Date : ..../..................../.................   Feeling: 😐😣😑😊😄

Today, I am grateful for _____

_____

_____

_____

_____

Positive Affirmations

I am _____

_____

_____

_____

_____

66 Favorite Quote **99**

Date : ..../..................../.................   Feeling: 😐😣😑😊😄

Today, I am grateful for _____

_____

_____

_____

_____

Positive Affirmations

I am _____

_____

_____

_____

_____

Date : ..../...................../....................   Feeling: 😊 😊 😊 😊 😊

Today, I am grateful for _____

_____

_____

_____

_____

Positive Affirmations

I am _____

_____

_____

_____

_____

66   Favorite Quote   99

Date : ..../...................../....................   Feeling: 😊 😊 😊 😊 😊

Today, I am grateful for _____

_____

_____

_____

_____

Positive Affirmations

I am _____

_____

_____

_____

_____

Date : ..../.............../...............   Feeling: 😞 😟 😐 🙂 😊
　　　　　　　　　　　　　　　　　　　　　　　　　　　　　　－ ～～～～～～ ＋

Today, I am grateful for _____

_____

_____

_____

_____

Positive Affirmations

I am _____

_____

_____

_____

_____

66   **Favorite Quote**   99

Date : ..../.............../...............   Feeling: 😞 😟 😐 🙂 😊
　　　　　　　　　　　　　　　　　　　　　　　　　　　　　　－ ～～～～～～ ＋

Today, I am grateful for _____

_____

_____

_____

_____

Positive Affirmations

I am _____

_____

_____

_____

_____

Date : ....../................../...................   Feeling: 😊😊😊😊😊
                                                                            − ▬▬▬▬▬ +

Today, I am grateful for _____

_____

_____

_____

_____

Positive Affirmations

I am _____

_____

_____

_____

_____

66   **Favorite Quote**   99

Date : ....../................../...................   Feeling: 😔😔😔😊😊
                                                                            − ▬▬▬▬▬ +

Today, I am grateful for _____

_____

_____

_____

_____

Positive Affirmations

I am _____

_____

_____

_____

_____

Date : ..../................../................   Feeling: 😖 😣 😐 🙂 😄
                                                            – ‹‹‹‹‹‹‹‹‹‹‹‹‹‹‹‹‹‹‹ +

Today, I am grateful for _____

_____

_____

_____

_____

                        Positive Affirmations
I am _____

_____

_____

_____

_____

66   Favorite Quote   99

Date : ..../................../................   Feeling: 😣 😐 😐 🙂 😄
                                                            – ‹‹‹‹‹‹‹‹‹‹‹‹‹‹‹‹‹‹‹ +

Today, I am grateful for _____

_____

_____

_____

_____

                        Positive Affirmations
I am _____

_____

_____

_____

_____

Date : ..../..................../.....................   Feeling: 😐😐😐😐😐

Today, I am grateful for _____

_____

_____

_____

_____

Positive Affirmations

I am _____

_____

_____

_____

_____

66   Favorite Quote   **99**

Date : ..../..................../.....................   Feeling: 😐😐😐😐😐

Today, I am grateful for _____

_____

_____

_____

_____

Positive Affirmations

I am _____

_____

_____

_____

_____

Ðate : ..../...................../................   Feeling: 😐 😐 😊 😊 😄
　　　　　　　　　　　　　　　　　　　　　　　　　　　　－ ▬▬▬▬▬ ＋

Today, I am grateful for _____

_____

_____

_____

_____

Positive Affirmations

I am _____

_____

_____

_____

_____

66　　　　　　Favorite Quote　　　　　　**99**

Ðate : ..../...................../................   Feeling: 😄 😐 😐 😊 😄
　　　　　　　　　　　　　　　　　　　　　　　　　　　　－ ▬▬▬▬▬ ＋

Today, I am grateful for _____

_____

_____

_____

_____

Positive Affirmations

I am _____

_____

_____

_____

_____

Date : ..../.........../.............. Feeling: 😣 😟 😐 🙂 😊
– ▬▬▬▬▬ +

Today, I am grateful for _____

_____

_____

_____

_____

Positive Affirmations

I am _____

_____

_____

_____

_____

" Favorite Quote **"**

Date : ..../.........../.............. Feeling: 😣 😟 😐 🙂 😊
– ▬▬▬▬▬ +

Today, I am grateful for _____

_____

_____

_____

_____

Positive Affirmations

I am _____

_____

_____

_____

_____

Date : ..../................./................   Feeling: 😐 😑 😐 🙂 😊

Today, I am grateful for _____

_____

_____

_____

_____

Positive Affirmations

I am _____

_____

_____

_____

_____

66 Favorite Quote 99

Date : ..../................./................   Feeling: 🙁 😐 😐 🙂 😊

Today, I am grateful for _____

_____

_____

_____

_____

Positive Affirmations

I am _____

_____

_____

_____

_____

Date : ..../............../................   Feeling: 😊 😐 😐 😊 😊

Today, I am grateful for _____

_____

_____

_____

_____

Positive Affirmations

I am _____

_____

_____

_____

_____

> **"** Favorite Quote **"**

Date : ..../............../................   Feeling: 😊 😐 😐 😊 😊

Today, I am grateful for _____

_____

_____

_____

_____

Positive Affirmations

I am _____

_____

_____

_____

_____

Date : ..../............../...............   Feeling: 😟 😐 😐 🙂 😊

Today, I am grateful for _____

_____

_____

_____

_____

Positive Affirmations

I am _____

_____

_____

_____

_____

❝ Favorite Quote ❞

Date : ..../............../...............   Feeling: 😟 😐 😐 🙂 😊

Today, I am grateful for _____

_____

_____

_____

_____

Positive Affirmations

I am _____

_____

_____

_____

_____

Date : ..../..................../..................   Feeling: 😣 😐 😐 😊 😄

Today, I am grateful for _____

_____

_____

_____

_____

Positive Affirmations

I am _____

_____

_____

_____

_____

66   Favorite Quote   **99**

Date : ..../..................../..................   Feeling: 😣 😐 😐 😊 😄

Today, I am grateful for _____

_____

_____

_____

_____

Positive Affirmations

I am _____

_____

_____

_____

_____

Date : ..../................/................   Feeling: 😐😐😐😊😊

Today, I am grateful for _____

_____

_____

_____

_____

Positive Affirmations

I am _____

_____

_____

_____

_____

66   Favorite Quote   **99**

Date : ..../................/................   Feeling: 😞😐😐😊😊

Today, I am grateful for _____

_____

_____

_____

_____

Positive Affirmations

I am _____

_____

_____

_____

_____

Date : ..../......../........   Feeling: 😩 😟 😐 🙂 😄
                                                  – ▬▬▬▬ +

Today, I am grateful for _____

_____

_____

_____

_____

Positive Affirmations

I am _____

_____

_____

_____

_____

66   Favorite Quote   99

Date : ..../......../........   Feeling: 😩 😟 😐 🙂 😄
                                                  – ▬▬▬▬ +

Today, I am grateful for _____

_____

_____

_____

_____

Positive Affirmations

I am _____

_____

_____

_____

_____

Date : ..../............./.................   Feeling: 😊 😐 😐 😊 😊

Today, I am grateful for _____

_____

_____

_____

_____

Positive Affirmations

I am _____

_____

_____

_____

_____

66 **Favorite Quote** 99

Date : ..../............./.................   Feeling: 😊 😐 😐 😊 😊

Today, I am grateful for _____

_____

_____

_____

_____

Positive Affirmations

I am _____

_____

_____

_____

_____

"One of the first signs of a spirit-filled life is enthusiasm."

— A. B. Simpson

Date : ..../................/................   Feeling: 😐 😑 😐 😊 😊

Today, I am grateful for _____

_____

_____

_____

_____

Positive Affirmations

I am _____

_____

_____

_____

_____

" Favorite Quote "

Date : ..../................/................   Feeling: 😐 😑 😐 😊 😊

Today, I am grateful for _____

_____

_____

_____

_____

Positive Affirmations

I am _____

_____

_____

_____

_____

Date : ..../................/................   Feeling: 😀😀😀😀😀
                                                                            − +

Today, I am grateful for _____

_____

_____

_____

_____

Positive Affirmations

I am _____

_____

_____

_____

_____

66   Favorite Quote   **99**

Date : ..../................/................   Feeling: 😀😀😀😀😀
                                                                            − +

Today, I am grateful for _____

_____

_____

_____

_____

Positive Affirmations

I am _____

_____

_____

_____

_____

Date : ..../................../................

Feeling:

Today, I am grateful for _____

_____

_____

_____

_____

Positive Affirmations

I am _____

_____

_____

_____

_____

66 Favorite Quote 99

Date : ..../................../................

Feeling:

Today, I am grateful for _____

_____

_____

_____

_____

Positive Affirmations

I am _____

_____

_____

_____

_____

Date : ..../................../................ Feeling: 😞 😟 😐 🙂 😊

Today, I am grateful for _____

_____

_____

_____

_____

Positive Affirmations

I am _____

_____

_____

_____

_____

66 Favorite Quote 99

Date : ..../................../................ Feeling: 😞 😟 😐 🙂 😊

Today, I am grateful for _____

_____

_____

_____

_____

Positive Affirmations

I am _____

_____

_____

_____

_____

Date : ..../................../................ Feeling: 😞 😐 😊 😄 😁
_ ———————————— +

Today, I am grateful for _____

_____

_____

_____

_____

Positive Affirmations

I am _____

_____

_____

_____

_____

66   Favorite Quote   99

Date : ..../................../................ Feeling: 😞 😐 😊 😄 😁
_ ———————————— +

Today, I am grateful for _____

_____

_____

_____

_____

Positive Affirmations

I am _____

_____

_____

_____

_____

Date : ..../.................../..................   Feeling: 😊 😐 😟 😣 😄
                                                                          – ▬▬▬▬▬ +

Today, I am grateful for _____

_____

_____

_____

_____

                        Positive Affirmations
I am _____

_____

_____

_____

_____

"   Favorite Quote   **"**

Date : ..../.................../..................   Feeling: 😣 😟 😐 😊 😄
                                                                          – ▬▬▬▬▬ +

Today, I am grateful for _____

_____

_____

_____

_____

                        Positive Affirmations
I am _____

_____

_____

_____

_____

Date : ..../.............../................   Feeling: 😖 😕 😐 🙂 😊

Today, I am grateful for _____

_____

_____

_____

_____

Positive Affirmations

I am _____

_____

_____

_____

_____

66   Favorite Quote   99

Date : ..../.............../................   Feeling: 😖 😕 😐 🙂 😊

Today, I am grateful for _____

_____

_____

_____

_____

Positive Affirmations

I am _____

_____

_____

_____

_____

Date : ..../..................../...................   Feeling: 😟 😕 😐 🙂 😊

Today, I am grateful for _____

_____

_____

_____

_____

Positive Affirmations

I am _____

_____

_____

_____

_____

66   Favorite Quote   **99**

Date : ..../..................../...................   Feeling: 😟 😕 😐 🙂 😊

Today, I am grateful for _____

_____

_____

_____

_____

Positive Affirmations

I am _____

_____

_____

_____

_____

Date : ..../................../................   Feeling: 😟 😐 😐 😊 😄

Today, I am grateful for _____

_____

_____

_____

_____

Positive Affirmations

I am _____

_____

_____

_____

_____

66   Favorite Quote   99

Date : ..../................../................   Feeling: 😟 😐 😐 😊 😄

Today, I am grateful for _____

_____

_____

_____

_____

Positive Affirmations

I am _____

_____

_____

_____

_____

Ðate : ..../...................../...................   Feeling: 😦 😦 😐 🙂 😊

Today, I am grateful for _____

_____

_____

_____

_____

Positive Affirmations

I am _____

_____

_____

_____

_____

66   Favorite Quote   99

Ðate : ..../...................../...................   Feeling: 😦 😦 😐 🙂 😊

Today, I am grateful for _____

_____

_____

_____

_____

Positive Affirmations

I am _____

_____

_____

_____

_____

Date : ..../................../................   Feeling: 😞 😕 😐 🙂 😄
‒ ▬▬▬▬▬▬▬ +

Today, I am grateful for _____

_____

_____

_____

_____

Positive Affirmations

I am _____

_____

_____

_____

_____

66 Favorite Quote **99**

Date : ..../................../................   Feeling: 😞 😕 😐 🙂 😄
‒ ▬▬▬▬▬▬▬ +

Today, I am grateful for _____

_____

_____

_____

_____

Positive Affirmations

I am _____

_____

_____

_____

_____

Date : ..../................../.................   Feeling: 😣 😐 😐 😐 😊
                                                              – ▬▬▬▬▬ +

Today, I am grateful for _____

_____

_____

_____

_____

Positive Affirmations

I am _____

_____

_____

_____

_____

66   Favorite Quote   99

Date : ..../................../.................   Feeling: 😣 😐 😐 😐 😊
                                                              – ▬▬▬▬▬ +

Today, I am grateful for _____

_____

_____

_____

_____

Positive Affirmations

I am _____

_____

_____

_____

_____

Date : ..../................./................   Feeling: 😟 😕 😐 🙂 😊
                                                             – ⚊⚊⚊⚊⚊ +

Today, I am grateful for _____

_____

_____

_____

_____

Positive Affirmations

I am _____

_____

_____

_____

_____

❝   Favorite Quote   ❞

Date : ..../................./................   Feeling: 😟 😕 😐 😐 🙂
                                                             – ⚊⚊⚊⚊⚊ +

Today, I am grateful for _____

_____

_____

_____

_____

Positive Affirmations

I am _____

_____

_____

_____

_____

Date : ..../....................../....................   Feeling: 😟 😐 😐 😐 😊

Today, I am grateful for _____

_____

_____

_____

_____

Positive Affirmations

I am _____

_____

_____

_____

_____

66 Favorite Quote **99**

Date : ..../....................../....................   Feeling: 😟 😐 😐 😐 😊

Today, I am grateful for _____

_____

_____

_____

_____

Positive Affirmations

I am _____

_____

_____

_____

_____

Date : ..../............../...............   Feeling: 😠 😐 😐 🙂 😊

Today, I am grateful for _____

_____

_____

_____

_____

Positive Affirmations

I am _____

_____

_____

_____

_____

❝   Favorite Quote   ❞

Date : ..../............../...............   Feeling: 😠 😐 😐 🙂 😊

Today, I am grateful for _____

_____

_____

_____

_____

Positive Affirmations

I am _____

_____

_____

_____

_____

Remember

"The best way to predict your future is to create it."

— Abraham Lincoln

Date : ..../.................../...................   Feeling: 😊😐😐😐😊

Today, I am grateful for _____

_____

_____

_____

_____

Positive Affirmations

I am _____

_____

_____

_____

_____

"   Favorite Quote   **"**

Date : ..../.................../...................   Feeling: 😊😐😐😐😊

Today, I am grateful for _____

_____

_____

_____

_____

Positive Affirmations

I am _____

_____

_____

_____

_____

Date : ..../...................../....................

Feeling:

Today, I am grateful for _____

_____

_____

_____

_____

Positive Affirmations

I am _____

_____

_____

_____

_____

66   Favorite Quote   99

Date : ..../...................../....................

Feeling:

Today, I am grateful for _____

_____

_____

_____

_____

Positive Affirmations

I am _____

_____

_____

_____

_____

Date : ..../............../................   Feeling: 😟 😣 😐 😊 😄

Today, I am grateful for _____

_____

_____

_____

_____

Positive Affirmations

I am _____

_____

_____

_____

_____

66   Favorite Quote   **99**

Date : ..../............../................   Feeling: 😟 😣 😐 😊 😄

Today, I am grateful for _____

_____

_____

_____

_____

Positive Affirmations

I am _____

_____

_____

_____

_____

Date : ..../................../................   Feeling: 😊 😐 😊 😐 😊
                                                                       -                    +

Today, I am grateful for _____

_____

_____

_____

_____

                        Positive Affirmations
I am _____

_____

_____

_____

_____

66   Favorite Quote   **99**

Date : ..../................../................   Feeling: 😊 😐 😐 😐 😊
                                                                       -                    +

Today, I am grateful for _____

_____

_____

_____

_____

                        Positive Affirmations
I am _____

_____

_____

_____

_____

Date : ..../................/................   Feeling: 😟 😐 😕 😊 😄

Today, I am grateful for _____

_____

_____

_____

_____

Positive Affirmations

I am _____

_____

_____

_____

_____

66   Favorite Quote   **99**

Date : ..../................/................   Feeling: 😟 😐 😕 😊 😄

Today, I am grateful for _____

_____

_____

_____

_____

Positive Affirmations

I am _____

_____

_____

_____

_____

Date : ..../.................../..................   Feeling: 😐😐😐😐😐
                                                                           – ▬▬▬▬ +

Today, I am grateful for _____

_____

_____

_____

_____

Positive Affirmations

I am _____

_____

_____

_____

_____

66   Favorite Quote   **99**

Date : ..../.................../..................   Feeling: 😐😐😐😐😐
                                                                           – ▬▬▬▬ +

Today, I am grateful for _____

_____

_____

_____

_____

Positive Affirmations

I am _____

_____

_____

_____

_____

Date : ..../..................../.................   Feeling: 😐 😑 😐 🙂 😊

Today, I am grateful for _____

_____

_____

_____

_____

Positive Affirmations

I am _____

_____

_____

_____

_____

66   Favorite Quote   **99**

Date : ..../..................../.................   Feeling: 😐 😑 😐 🙂 😊

Today, I am grateful for _____

_____

_____

_____

_____

Positive Affirmations

I am _____

_____

_____

_____

_____

Date : ..../................/................   Feeling: 😟 😔 😐 🙂 😄
‒ ▬▬▬▬▬▬▬ +

Today, I am grateful for _____

_____

_____

_____

_____

Positive Affirmations

I am _____

_____

_____

_____

_____

66   Favorite Quote   99

Date : ..../................/................   Feeling: 😟 😔 😐 🙂 😄
‒ ▬▬▬▬▬▬▬ +

Today, I am grateful for _____

_____

_____

_____

_____

Positive Affirmations

I am _____

_____

_____

_____

_____

Date : ..../................./................ Feeling: 😞 😣 😐 😊 😄

Today, I am grateful for _____

_____

_____

_____

_____

Positive Affirmations

I am _____

_____

_____

_____

_____

❝ Favorite Quote ❞

Date : ..../................./................ Feeling: 😞 😣 😐 😊 😄

Today, I am grateful for _____

_____

_____

_____

_____

Positive Affirmations

I am _____

_____

_____

_____

_____

Date : ..../..................../...................   Feeling: 😣 😟 😐 🙂 😄
                                                                  – ▱▱▱▱▱ +

Today, I am grateful for _____

_____

_____

_____

_____

Positive Affirmations

I am _____

_____

_____

_____

_____

> 66   **Favorite Quote**   99

Date : ..../..................../...................   Feeling: 😣 😟 😐 🙂 😄
                                                                  – ▱▱▱▱▱ +

Today, I am grateful for _____

_____

_____

_____

_____

Positive Affirmations

I am _____

_____

_____

_____

_____

Date : ..../................/................   Feeling: 😟 😐 😐 😊 😄 − ~~~~~~~~ +

Today, I am grateful for _____

_____

_____

_____

_____

Positive Affirmations

I am _____

_____

_____

_____

_____

66   Favorite Quote   99

Date : ..../................/................   Feeling: 😟 😐 😐 😊 😄 − ~~~~~~~~ +

Today, I am grateful for _____

_____

_____

_____

_____

Positive Affirmations

I am _____

_____

_____

_____

_____

Date : ..../..................../................   Feeling: 😖 😣 😐 😕 😊

$Today, I am grateful for$ _____

_____

_____

_____

_____

Positive Affirmations

$I am$ _____

_____

_____

_____

_____

❝   Favorite Quote   ❞

Date : ..../..................../................   Feeling: 😖 😣 😐 😕 😊

$Today, I am grateful for$ _____

_____

_____

_____

_____

Positive Affirmations

$I am$ _____

_____

_____

_____

_____

Date : ..../.........../.............   Feeling: 😟 😐 😕 🙂 😊

Today, I am grateful for _____

_____

_____

_____

_____

Positive Affirmations

I am _____

_____

_____

_____

_____

66   Favorite Quote   **99**

Date : ..../.........../.............   Feeling: 😟 😐 😕 🙂 😊

Today, I am grateful for _____

_____

_____

_____

_____

Positive Affirmations

I am _____

_____

_____

_____

_____

Date : ..../...................../..................   Feeling: 😀 😀 😀 😀 😀

Today, I am grateful for _____

_____

_____

_____

_____

Positive Affirmations

I am _____

_____

_____

_____

_____

❝   Favorite Quote   ❞

Date : ..../...................../..................   Feeling: 😠 😐 😐 😐 😊

Today, I am grateful for _____

_____

_____

_____

_____

Positive Affirmations

I am _____

_____

_____

_____

_____

Date : ..../................../.................

Feeling: 😐 😕 🙂 😊 😄

Today, I am grateful for _____

_____

_____

_____

_____

Positive Affirmations

I am _____

_____

_____

_____

_____

" **Favorite Quote** "

Date : ..../................../.................

Feeling: 😐 😕 🙂 😊 😄

Today, I am grateful for _____

_____

_____

_____

_____

Positive Affirmations

I am _____

_____

_____

_____

_____

"Knowing is not enough; we must apply. Willing is not enough; we must do."

— Johann Wolfgang von Goethe

Ðate : ..../................/................   Feeling: 😊😑😑😊😊

Today, I am grateful for _____

_____

_____

_____

_____

Positive Affirmations

I am _____

_____

_____

_____

_____

> ## Favorite Quote

Ðate : ..../................/................   Feeling: 😊😑😑😊😊

Today, I am grateful for _____

_____

_____

_____

_____

Positive Affirmations

I am _____

_____

_____

_____

_____

Date : ..../...................../.................

Feeling: 😟 😐 🙂 😊 😁 − ▬▬▬▬ +

Today, I am grateful for _____

_____

_____

_____

_____

Positive Affirmations

I am _____

_____

_____

_____

_____

" Favorite Quote **"**

Date : ..../...................../.................

Feeling: 😟 😐 😐 🙂 😊 − ▬▬▬▬ +

Today, I am grateful for _____

_____

_____

_____

_____

Positive Affirmations

I am _____

_____

_____

_____

_____

Date : ..../................../................   Feeling: 😀😀😀😀😀

Today, I am grateful for _____

_____

_____

_____

_____

Positive Affirmations

I am _____

_____

_____

_____

_____

66   Favorite Quote   99

Date : ..../................../................   Feeling: 😀😀😀😀😀

Today, I am grateful for _____

_____

_____

_____

_____

Positive Affirmations

I am _____

_____

_____

_____

_____

Date : ..../.................../...................

Feeling:

Today, I am grateful for _____

_____

_____

_____

_____

Positive Affirmations

I am _____

_____

_____

_____

_____

66 Favorite Quote 99

Date : ..../.................../...................

Feeling:

Today, I am grateful for _____

_____

_____

_____

_____

Positive Affirmations

I am _____

_____

_____

_____

_____

Date : ..../................./................　　　　　　　Feeling: 😦 😑 😐 😕 🙂

Today, I am grateful for _____

_____

_____

_____

_____

Positive Affirmations

I am

_____

_____

_____

_____

" Favorite Quote "

Date : ..../................./................　　　　　　　Feeling: 😦 😑 😐 😕 🙂

Today, I am grateful for _____

_____

_____

_____

_____

Positive Affirmations

I am

_____

_____

_____

_____

Date : ..../................../..................   Feeling: 😣 😟 😐 🙂 😄
                                                                        − +

Today, I am grateful for _____

_____

_____

_____

_____

Positive Affirmations

I am _____

_____

_____

_____

_____

66   Favorite Quote   99

Date : ..../................../..................   Feeling: 😣 😟 😐 😐 🙂
                                                                        − +

Today, I am grateful for _____

_____

_____

_____

_____

Positive Affirmations

I am _____

_____

_____

_____

_____

Date : ..../................./................   Feeling: 😐😒😐😊😄 − ~~~~~~~ +

Today, I am grateful for _____

_____

_____

_____

_____

Positive Affirmations

I am _____

_____

_____

_____

_____

66   Favorite Quote   99

Date : ..../................./................   Feeling: 😒😐😒😊😄 − ~~~~~~~ +

Today, I am grateful for _____

_____

_____

_____

_____

Positive Affirmations

I am _____

_____

_____

_____

_____

Date : ..../.................../................

Feeling: ☺ ☺ ☺ ☺ ☺
− +

Today, I am grateful for _____

_____

_____

_____

_____

Positive Affirmations

I am _____

_____

_____

_____

_____

" Favorite Quote "

Date : ..../.................../................

Feeling: ☺ ☺ ☺ ☺ ☺
− +

Today, I am grateful for _____

_____

_____

_____

_____

Positive Affirmations

I am _____

_____

_____

_____

_____

Date : ..../............../.................   Feeling: 😞 😐 😊 😊 😄
                                                                      – ▬▬▬▬▬▬▬ +

Today, I am grateful for _____

_____

_____

_____

_____

                         Positive Affirmations
I am _____

_____

_____

_____

_____

66   Favorite Quote   **99**

Date : ..../............../.................   Feeling: 😞 😐 😐 😊 😄
                                                                      – ▬▬▬▬▬▬▬ +

Today, I am grateful for _____

_____

_____

_____

_____

                         Positive Affirmations
I am _____

_____

_____

_____

_____

Date : ..../................../..................   Feeling: 😣 😕 😐 🙂 😊

Today, I am grateful for _____

_____

_____

_____

_____

Positive Affirmations

I am _____

_____

_____

_____

_____

66   Favorite Quote   99

Date : ..../................../..................   Feeling: 😣 😕 😐 🙂 😊

Today, I am grateful for _____

_____

_____

_____

_____

Positive Affirmations

I am _____

_____

_____

_____

_____

Đate : ..../..................../.................   Feeling: 😟😐😐😊😊

Today, I am grateful for _____

_____

_____

_____

_____

Positive Affirmations

I am _____

_____

_____

_____

_____

66   Favorite Quote   99

Đate : ..../..................../.................   Feeling: 😟😐😐😊😊

Today, I am grateful for _____

_____

_____

_____

_____

Positive Affirmations

I am _____

_____

_____

_____

_____

Date : ..../................../.................

Feeling:

Today, I am grateful for _____

_____

_____

_____

_____

Positive Affirmations

I am _____

_____

_____

_____

_____

66   Favorite Quote   99

Date : ..../................../.................

Feeling:

Today, I am grateful for _____

_____

_____

_____

_____

Positive Affirmations

I am _____

_____

_____

_____

_____

Date : ..../................../................ Feeling: 😊 😊 😊 😊 😊

Today, I am grateful for _____

_____

_____

_____

_____

Positive Affirmations

I am _____

_____

_____

_____

_____

" Favorite Quote "

Date : ..../................../................ Feeling: 😊 😊 😊 😊 😊

Today, I am grateful for _____

_____

_____

_____

_____

Positive Affirmations

I am _____

_____

_____

_____

_____

Date : ..../...................../...................   Feeling: 😊 😊 😐 😊 😊

Today, I am grateful for _____

_____

_____

_____

_____

Positive Affirmations

I am _____

_____

_____

_____

_____

66   Favorite Quote   99

Date : ..../...................../...................   Feeling: 😞 😐 😐 😐 😊

Today, I am grateful for _____

_____

_____

_____

_____

Positive Affirmations

I am _____

_____

_____

_____

_____

Date : ..../........../..............   Feeling: 😐 😟 😐 😊 😊

Today, I am grateful for _____

_____

_____

_____

_____

Positive Affirmations

I am _____

_____

_____

_____

_____

Date : ..../........../..............   Feeling: 😊 😟 😐 😊 😊

Today, I am grateful for _____

_____

_____

_____

_____

Positive Affirmations

I am _____

_____

_____

_____

_____

"Your mind will give back exactly what you put into it."

— James Joyce

Date : ..../................/.................   Feeling: 😣 😣 😐 😊 😄 _ ▬▬▬▬▬ +

Today, I am grateful for _____

_____

_____

_____

_____

Positive Affirmations

I am _____

_____

_____

_____

_____

❝   Favorite Quote   ❞

Date : ..../................/.................   Feeling: 😣 😣 😐 😊 😄 _ ▬▬▬▬▬ +

Today, I am grateful for _____

_____

_____

_____

_____

Positive Affirmations

I am _____

_____

_____

_____

_____

Date : ..../................/................   Feeling: 😫 😐 🙂 😀 😄
                                                                    – ▬▬▬▬▬▬ +

Today, I am grateful for _____

_____

_____

_____

_____

Positive Affirmations

I am _____

_____

_____

_____

_____

66   Favorite Quote   **99**

Date : ..../................/................   Feeling: 😫 😐 😐 🙂 😄
                                                                    – ▬▬▬▬▬▬ +

Today, I am grateful for _____

_____

_____

_____

_____

Positive Affirmations

I am _____

_____

_____

_____

_____

Date : ..../.................../................   Feeling: 😠 😞 😐 🙂 😄

Today, I am grateful for _____

_____

_____

_____

_____

Positive Affirmations

I am _____

_____

_____

_____

_____

" Favorite Quote "

Date : ..../.................../................   Feeling: 😠 😞 😐 🙂 😄

Today, I am grateful for _____

_____

_____

_____

_____

Positive Affirmations

I am _____

_____

_____

_____

_____

Date : ..../......................./.......................

Feeling:

Today, I am grateful for _____

_____

_____

_____

_____

Positive Affirmations

I am _____

_____

_____

_____

_____

66 **Favorite Quote** 99

Date : ..../......................./.......................

Feeling:

Today, I am grateful for _____

_____

_____

_____

_____

Positive Affirmations

I am _____

_____

_____

_____

_____

Date : ..../..................../................ Feeling:

Today, I am grateful for _____

_____

_____

_____

_____

Positive Affirmations

I am _____

_____

_____

_____

_____

" Favorite Quote "

Date : ..../..................../................ Feeling:

Today, I am grateful for _____

_____

_____

_____

_____

Positive Affirmations

I am _____

_____

_____

_____

_____

Date : ..../..................../....................   Feeling: 😐 😐 😐 😐 😊

Today, I am grateful for _____

_____

_____

_____

_____

Positive Affirmations

I am _____

_____

_____

_____

_____

66   Favorite Quote   **99**

Date : ..../..................../....................   Feeling: 😐 😐 😐 😐 😊

Today, I am grateful for _____

_____

_____

_____

_____

Positive Affirmations

I am _____

_____

_____

_____

_____

Date : ..../................../................   Feeling: 😊 😊 😊 😊 😊
                                                              – ▬▬▬▬▬▬▬ +

Today, I am grateful for _____

_____

_____

_____

_____

                    Positive Affirmations
I am _____

_____

_____

_____

_____

❝   Favorite Quote   ❞

Date : ..../................../................   Feeling: 😊 😊 😊 😊 😊
                                                              – ▬▬▬▬▬▬▬ +

Today, I am grateful for _____

_____

_____

_____

_____

                    Positive Affirmations
I am _____

_____

_____

_____

_____

Date : ..../..................../....................   Feeling: 😊 😊 😊 😊 😊

Today, I am grateful for _____

_____

_____

_____

_____

Positive Affirmations

I am _____

_____

_____

_____

_____

> ❝ Favorite Quote ❞

Date : ..../..................../....................   Feeling: 😊 😊 😊 😊 😊

Today, I am grateful for _____

_____

_____

_____

_____

Positive Affirmations

I am _____

_____

_____

_____

_____

Date : ..../................../...............   Feeling: 😀 😟 😐 😐 😊
‾ ▬▬▬▬▬▬▬ ₊

𝒯oday, 𝒥 am grateful for _____

_____

_____

_____

_____

Positive Affirmations

𝒥 am _____

_____

_____

_____

_____

❝   Favorite Quote   ❞

Date : ..../................../...............   Feeling: 😀 😟 😐 😐 😊
‾ ▬▬▬▬▬▬▬ ₊

𝒯oday, 𝒥 am grateful for _____

_____

_____

_____

_____

Positive Affirmations

𝒥 am _____

_____

_____

_____

_____

Date : ..../.............../...............   Feeling: 😐 😐 😐 😐 😀

Today, I am grateful for _____

_____

_____

_____

_____

Positive Affirmations

I am _____

_____

_____

_____

_____

66   Favorite Quote   **99**

Date : ..../.............../...............   Feeling: 😐 😐 😐 😐 😀

Today, I am grateful for _____

_____

_____

_____

_____

Positive Affirmations

I am _____

_____

_____

_____

_____

Date : ..../................../.................. Feeling: 🙁🙁🙂🙂😊
− ▬▬▬▬▬▬▬ +

Today, I am grateful for _____

_____

_____

_____

_____

Positive Affirmations

I am _____

_____

_____

_____

_____

❝ Favorite Quote ❞

Date : ..../................../.................. Feeling: 🙁🙁🙂🙂😊
− ▬▬▬▬▬▬▬ +

Today, I am grateful for _____

_____

_____

_____

_____

Positive Affirmations

I am _____

_____

_____

_____

_____

Date : ..../............../.............   Feeling: 😐😐😐😐😐

Today, I am grateful for _____

_____

_____

_____

_____

Positive Affirmations

I am _____

_____

_____

_____

_____

66   Favorite Quote   99

Date : ..../............../.............   Feeling: 😐😐😐😐😐

Today, I am grateful for _____

_____

_____

_____

_____

Positive Affirmations

I am _____

_____

_____

_____

_____

Date : ..../................/................   Feeling: 😟 😐 😐 🙂 😊

Today, I am grateful for _____

_____

_____

_____

_____

Positive Affirmations

I am _____

_____

_____

_____

_____

66   Favorite Quote   **99**

Date : ..../................/................   Feeling: 😟 😐 😐 🙂 😊

Today, I am grateful for _____

_____

_____

_____

_____

Positive Affirmations

I am _____

_____

_____

_____

_____

Date : ..../................./................. Feeling: ☺ ☺ ☺ ☺ ☺
                                                    _ ~~~~~~~~~~~ +

Today, I am grateful for _____

_____

_____

_____

_____

_____

Positive Affirmations

I am _____

_____

_____

_____

_____

66   Favorite Quote   **99**

Date : ..../................./................. Feeling: ☹ ☹ ☺ ☺ ☺
                                                    _ ~~~~~~~~~~~ +

Today, I am grateful for _____

_____

_____

_____

_____

Positive Affirmations

I am _____

_____

_____

_____

_____

Date : ..../..................../..................   Feeling: 😐 😦 😐 😊 😄

Today, I am grateful for _____

_____

_____

_____

_____

Positive Affirmations

I am _____

_____

_____

_____

_____

66   Favorite Quote   99

Date : ..../..................../..................   Feeling: 😄 😦 😐 😦 😊

Today, I am grateful for _____

_____

_____

_____

_____

Positive Affirmations

I am _____

_____

_____

_____

_____

Remember

"Positive anything is better than negative nothing."

— Elbert Hubbard

Date : ..../................../................   Feeling: 😊 😐 😣 😊 😊
                                                                 − ▬▬▬▬▬ +

Today, I am grateful for _____

_____

_____

_____

_____

                    Positive Affirmations
I am _____

_____

_____

_____

_____

66   Favorite Quote   **99**

Date : ..../................../................   Feeling: 😊 😐 😣 😊 😊
                                                                 − ▬▬▬▬▬ +

Today, I am grateful for _____

_____

_____

_____

_____

                    Positive Affirmations
I am _____

_____

_____

_____

_____

Date : ..../.................../..................   Feeling: 😣 😟 😐 🙂 😄
                                                                  – ▬▬▬▬▬▬▬▬ +

Today, I am grateful for _____

_____

_____

_____

_____

                              Positive Affirmations

I am _____

_____

_____

_____

_____

❝   Favorite Quote   ❞

Date : ..../.................../..................   Feeling: 😣 😟 😐 🙂 😄
                                                                  – ▬▬▬▬▬▬▬▬ +

Today, I am grateful for _____

_____

_____

_____

                              Positive Affirmations

I am _____

_____

_____

_____

_____

Date : ..../................../................   Feeling: 😟 😕 😐 🙂 😊

Today, I am grateful for _____

_____

_____

_____

_____

Positive Affirmations

_I am_ _____

_____

_____

_____

_____

> ## Favorite Quote

Date : ..../................../................   Feeling: 😟 😕 😐 🙂 😊

Today, I am grateful for _____

_____

_____

_____

_____

Positive Affirmations

_I am_ _____

_____

_____

_____

_____

Date : ..../..................../.................... Feeling: ☹ ☹ ☺ ☺ ☺

Today, I am grateful for _____

_____

_____

_____

_____

Positive Affirmations

_I am_ _____

_____

_____

_____

_____

" Favorite Quote "

Date : ..../..................../.................... Feeling: ☹ ☹ ☺ ☺ ☺

Today, I am grateful for _____

_____

_____

_____

_____

Positive Affirmations

_I am_ _____

_____

_____

_____

_____

Date : ..../................../................   Feeling: 😠😕😐🙂😊

Today, I am grateful for _____

_____

_____

_____

_____

Positive Affirmations

I am _____

_____

_____

_____

_____

66   Favorite Quote   99

Date : ..../................../................   Feeling: 😠😕😐🙂😊

Today, I am grateful for _____

_____

_____

_____

_____

Positive Affirmations

I am _____

_____

_____

_____

_____

Date : ..../....................../....................   Feeling: 😊😊😊😊😊

Today, I am grateful for _____

_____

_____

_____

_____

Positive Affirmations

I am _____

_____

_____

_____

_____

" Favorite Quote "

Date : ..../....................../....................   Feeling: 😊😊😊😊😊

Today, I am grateful for _____

_____

_____

_____

_____

Positive Affirmations

I am _____

_____

_____

_____

_____

Date : ..../..................../.................   Feeling: 😐 😐 😐 😊 😊

Today, I am grateful for _____

_____

_____

_____

_____

Positive Affirmations

I am _____

_____

_____

_____

_____

" **Favorite Quote** "

Date : ..../..................../.................   Feeling: 😐 😐 😐 😊 😊

Today, I am grateful for _____

_____

_____

_____

_____

Positive Affirmations

I am _____

_____

_____

_____

_____

Date : ..../................./................   Feeling: 😊 😐 😐 😐 😊
                                                            – ▭▭▭▭▭▭ +

Today, I am grateful for _____

_____

_____

_____

_____

Positive Affirmations

I am _____

_____

_____

_____

_____

66   Favorite Quote   **99**

Date : ..../................./................   Feeling: 😊 😐 😐 😐 😊
                                                            – ▭▭▭▭▭▭ +

Today, I am grateful for _____

_____

_____

_____

_____

Positive Affirmations

I am _____

_____

_____

_____

_____

Date : ..../.........../.................. Feeling: 😞😐🙂😊😄

Today, I am grateful for _____

_____

_____

_____

_____

Positive Affirmations

I am _____

_____

_____

_____

_____

66 Favorite Quote 99

Date : ..../.........../.................. Feeling: 😞😐🙂😊😄

Today, I am grateful for _____

_____

_____

_____

_____

Positive Affirmations

I am _____

_____

_____

_____

_____

Date : ..../..................../...................   Feeling: 😞 😟 😐 🙂 😄

Today, I am grateful for _____

_____

_____

_____

_____

Positive Affirmations

I am _____

_____

_____

_____

_____

❝ Favorite Quote **❞**

Date : ..../..................../...................   Feeling: 😞 😟 😐 🙂 😄

Today, I am grateful for _____

_____

_____

_____

_____

Positive Affirmations

I am _____

_____

_____

_____

_____

Date : ..../....................../.................   Feeling: 😀 😒 😐 😊 😄
                                                                              – ▬▬▬▬▬▬▬▬▬ +

Today, I am grateful for _____

_____

_____

_____

_____

                         Positive Affirmations

I am _____

_____

_____

_____

_____

66   Favorite Quote   **99**

Date : ..../....................../.................   Feeling: 😀 😒 😐 😊 😄
                                                                              – ▬▬▬▬▬▬▬▬▬ +

Today, I am grateful for _____

_____

_____

_____

_____

                         Positive Affirmations

I am _____

_____

_____

_____

_____

Date : ..../................../.................   Feeling: ☹ 😐 😐 😐 🙂

Today, I am grateful for _____

_____

_____

_____

_____

Positive Affirmations

I am _____

_____

_____

_____

_____

66   Favorite Quote   99

Date : ..../................../.................   Feeling: 😐 😐 😐 😐 🙂

Today, I am grateful for _____

_____

_____

_____

_____

Positive Affirmations

I am _____

_____

_____

_____

_____

Date : ..../................../................   Feeling: 😐 😦 😐 😊 😄

Today, I am grateful for _____

_____

_____

_____

_____

Positive Affirmations

I am _____

_____

_____

_____

_____

❝ Favorite Quote ❞

Date : ..../................../................   Feeling: 😦 😦 😐 😊 😄

Today, I am grateful for _____

_____

_____

_____

_____

Positive Affirmations

I am _____

_____

_____

_____

_____

Date : ....../............../...............   Feeling: 😐😐😐😐😐

Today, I am grateful for _____

_____

_____

_____

_____

Positive Affirmations

I am _____

_____

_____

_____

_____

" Favorite Quote "

Date : ....../............../...............   Feeling: 😐😐😐😐😐

Today, I am grateful for _____

_____

_____

_____

_____

Positive Affirmations

I am _____

_____

_____

_____

Date : ..../..................../................

Feeling:

Today, I am grateful for _____

_____

_____

_____

_____

Positive Affirmations

I am _____

_____

_____

_____

_____

" Favorite Quote **"**

Date : ..../..................../................

Feeling:

Today, I am grateful for _____

_____

_____

_____

_____

Positive Affirmations

I am _____

_____

_____

_____

_____

"He who has health, has hope; and he who has hope, has everything. "

— Thomas Carlyle

Date : ..../................../................   Feeling: 😞 😐 😶 🙂 😊
 − ▬▬▬▬▬ +

Today, I am grateful for _____

_____

_____

_____

_____

Positive Affirmations

I am
_____

_____

_____

_____

_____

❝ Favorite Quote **❞**

Date : ..../................../................   Feeling: 😞 😐 😶 🙂 😊
 − ▬▬▬▬▬ +

Today, I am grateful for _____

_____

_____

_____

_____

Positive Affirmations

I am
_____

_____

_____

_____

_____

Date : .... / .... / ....   Feeling: 😊😊😊😊😊 _ ———————— +

Today, I am grateful for _____

_____

_____

_____

_____

Positive Affirmations

I am _____

_____

_____

_____

_____

66   Favorite Quote   99

Date : .... / .... / ....   Feeling: 😞😐😐😐😊 _ ———————— +

Today, I am grateful for _____

_____

_____

_____

_____

Positive Affirmations

I am _____

_____

_____

_____

_____

Date : ..../....................../....................   Feeling: 😐 😦 😐 😊 😄

Today, I am grateful for _____

_____

_____

_____

_____

Positive Affirmations

I am _____

_____

_____

_____

_____

66   Favorite Quote   99

Date : ..../....................../....................   Feeling: 😦 😦 😐 😊 😄

Today, I am grateful for _____

_____

_____

_____

_____

Positive Affirmations

I am _____

_____

_____

_____

_____

Date : ..../..................../..................   Feeling: 😀 😊 😐 😕 😄

Today, I am grateful for _____

_____

_____

_____

_____

_____

Positive Affirmations

I am _____

_____

_____

_____

_____

66   Favorite Quote   **99**

Date : ..../..................../..................   Feeling: 😦 😐 😐 😐 😊

Today, I am grateful for _____

_____

_____

_____

_____

Positive Affirmations

I am _____

_____

_____

_____

_____

Date : ..../..................../................ Feeling: 😫 😟 😐 🙂 😊 − +

Today, I am grateful for _____

_____

_____

_____

_____

Positive Affirmations

I am _____

_____

_____

_____

_____

" Favorite Quote "

Date : ..../..................../................ Feeling: 😫 😟 😐 🙂 😊 − +

Today, I am grateful for _____

_____

_____

_____

_____

Positive Affirmations

I am _____

_____

_____

_____

_____

Date : ..../..................../.................

Feeling: ☹ 😐 😐 🙂 😊

Today, I am grateful for _____

_____

_____

_____

_____

Positive Affirmations

I am _____

_____

_____

_____

_____

66   Favorite Quote   99

Date : ..../..................../.................

Feeling: ☹ 😐 😐 🙂 😊

Today, I am grateful for _____

_____

_____

_____

_____

Positive Affirmations

I am _____

_____

_____

_____

_____

Date : ..../....................../....................   Feeling: 😊 😣 😐 😊 😄

Today, I am grateful for _____

_____

_____

_____

_____

Positive Affirmations

I am _____

_____

_____

_____

_____

> ❝ **Favorite Quote** ❞

Date : ..../....................../....................   Feeling: 😊 😣 😐 😊 😄

Today, I am grateful for _____

_____

_____

_____

_____

Positive Affirmations

I am _____

_____

_____

_____

_____

Date : ..../................../................   Feeling: 😊😊😊😊😊

Today, I am grateful for _____

_____

_____

_____

_____

_____

Positive Affirmations

I am _____

_____

_____

_____

_____

_____

" Favorite Quote "

Date : ..../................../................   Feeling: 😊😊😊😊😊

Today, I am grateful for _____

_____

_____

_____

_____

Positive Affirmations

I am _____

_____

_____

_____

_____

Date : ..../................../................

Feeling: 😠 😦 😐 🙂 😊 − ▬▬▬▬▬ +

Today, I am grateful for _____

_____

_____

_____

_____

Positive Affirmations

I am _____

_____

_____

_____

_____

66 Favorite Quote **99**

Date : ..../................../................

Feeling: 😠 😦 😐 🙂 😊 − ▬▬▬▬▬ +

Today, I am grateful for _____

_____

_____

_____

_____

Positive Affirmations

I am _____

_____

_____

_____

_____

Date : ..../......../........   Feeling: 😞 😟 😐 🙁 😊

Today, I am grateful for _____

_____

_____

_____

_____

Positive Affirmations

I am _____

_____

_____

_____

_____

_____

" Favorite Quote "

Date : ..../......../........   Feeling: 😞 😟 😐 🙁 😊

Today, I am grateful for _____

_____

_____

_____

_____

Positive Affirmations

I am _____

_____

_____

_____

_____

Date : ..../................../..................   Feeling: 😟 😐 😐 😊 😄

Today, I am grateful for _____

_____

_____

_____

_____

Positive Affirmations

I am _____

_____

_____

_____

_____

> **" "**   **Favorite Quote**   **" "**

Date : ..../................../..................   Feeling: 😟 😐 😐 😊 😄

Today, I am grateful for _____

_____

_____

_____

_____

Positive Affirmations

I am _____

_____

_____

_____

_____

Date : ..../..................../................ Feeling: 😊 😊 😊 😊 😊

Today, I am grateful for _____

_____

_____

_____

_____

Positive Affirmations

I am _____

_____

_____

_____

_____

66 Favorite Quote **99**

Date : ..../..................../................ Feeling: 😊 😊 😊 😊 😊

Today, I am grateful for _____

_____

_____

_____

_____

Positive Affirmations

I am _____

_____

_____

_____

_____

Date : ..../................../................   Feeling: 😐😐😐😐😐

Today, I am grateful for _____

_____

_____

_____

_____

Positive Affirmations

I am _____

_____

_____

_____

_____

66   **Favorite Quote**   99

Date : ..../................../................   Feeling: 😐😐😐😐😐

Today, I am grateful for _____

_____

_____

_____

_____

Positive Affirmations

I am _____

_____

_____

_____

_____

Date : .... / .... / ....   Feeling: 😊 😊 😊 😊 😊

Today, I am grateful for _____

_____

_____

_____

_____

Positive Affirmations

I am _____

_____

_____

_____

_____

66   Favorite Quote   99

Date : .... / .... / ....   Feeling: 😟 😐 😐 😊 😊

Today, I am grateful for _____

_____

_____

_____

Positive Affirmations

I am _____

_____

_____

_____

Date : ..../................../................ Feeling: 😠 😟 😐 🙂 😊
– ▬▬▬▬▬ +

Today, I am grateful for _____

_____

_____

_____

_____

Positive Affirmations

I am _____

_____

_____

_____

_____

❝ Favorite Quote ❞

Date : ..../................../................ Feeling: 😠 😟 😐 🙂 😊
– ▬▬▬▬▬ +

Today, I am grateful for _____

_____

_____

_____

_____

Positive Affirmations

I am _____

_____

_____

_____

_____

Remember

"The best way to make your dreams come true is to wake up."

— Paul Valery

Date : ..../..................../...................   Feeling: 😟😠😐😊😄

Today, I am grateful for _____

_____

_____

_____

_____

Positive Affirmations

I am _____

_____

_____

_____

_____

❝ Favorite Quote **❞**

Date : ..../..................../...................   Feeling: 😟😠😐😐😊

Today, I am grateful for _____

_____

_____

_____

_____

Positive Affirmations

I am _____

_____

_____

_____

_____

Date : ..../................./.................   Feeling: 😟 😐 😐 😊 😄

Today, I am grateful for _____

_____

_____

_____

_____

Positive Affirmations

I am _____

_____

_____

_____

_____

66   Favorite Quote   99

Date : ..../................./.................   Feeling: 😟 😐 😐 😊 😄

Today, I am grateful for _____

_____

_____

_____

_____

Positive Affirmations

I am _____

_____

_____

_____

_____

Date : ..../.................../...................   Feeling: 😟 😕 😐 🙂 😄

Today, I am grateful for _____

_____

_____

_____

_____

Positive Affirmations

I am _____

_____

_____

_____

_____

"   Favorite Quote   **"**

Date : ..../.................../...................   Feeling: 😟 😕 😐 🙂 😄

Today, I am grateful for _____

_____

_____

_____

_____

Positive Affirmations

I am _____

_____

_____

_____

_____

Date : ..../............../.............   Feeling: 😊 😊 😊 😊 😊
                                                                              – ———————— +

Today, I am grateful for _____

_____

_____

_____

_____

                              Positive Affirmations
I am _____

_____

_____

_____

_____

66   Favorite Quote   **99**

Date : ..../............../.............   Feeling: 😣 😐 😐 😐 😊
                                                                              – ———————— +

Today, I am grateful for _____

_____

_____

_____

_____

                              Positive Affirmations
I am _____

_____

_____

_____

_____

Ðate : ..../...................../...................   Feeling: 😟 😕 😐 🙂 😊

Today, I am grateful for _____

_____

_____

_____

_____

Positive Affirmations

I am _____

_____

_____

_____

_____

66   Favorite Quote   99

Ðate : ..../...................../...................   Feeling: 😟 😕 😐 🙂 😊

Today, I am grateful for _____

_____

_____

_____

_____

Positive Affirmations

I am _____

_____

_____

_____

_____

Date : ..../................/................   Feeling: 😐😐😐😐😐
                                                                    −   +

Today, I am grateful for _____

_____

_____

_____

_____

Positive Affirmations

I am _____

_____

_____

_____

_____

❝   Favorite Quote   **❞**

Date : ..../................/................   Feeling: 😐😐😐😐😐
                                                                    −   +

Today, I am grateful for _____

_____

_____

_____

_____

Positive Affirmations

I am _____

_____

_____

_____

_____

Date : ..../................../................   Feeling: 😐😟😐😐😊

Today, I am grateful for _____

_____

_____

_____

_____

Positive Affirmations

I am _____

_____

_____

_____

_____

66   Favorite Quote   **99**

Date : ..../................../................   Feeling: 😊😟😐😐😊

Today, I am grateful for _____

_____

_____

_____

_____

Positive Affirmations

I am _____

_____

_____

_____

_____

Date : ..../...................../....................   Feeling: 😣 😟 😐 😊 😄

Today, I am grateful for _____

_____

_____

_____

_____

Positive Affirmations

_I am_ _____

_____

_____

_____

_____

❝   Favorite Quote   ❞

Date : ..../...................../....................   Feeling: 😣 😟 😐 😟 😊

Today, I am grateful for _____

_____

_____

_____

_____

Positive Affirmations

_I am_ _____

_____

_____

_____

_____

Date : ..../........./............   Feeling: 😄 😐 😊 😊 😄
                                                                   − ▭▭▭▭▭▭ +

Today, I am grateful for _____

_____

_____

_____

_____

Positive Affirmations

I am _____

_____

_____

_____

_____

❝   Favorite Quote   ❞

Date : ..../........./............   Feeling: 😄 😐 😊 😊 😄
                                                                   − ▭▭▭▭▭▭ +

Today, I am grateful for _____

_____

_____

_____

_____

Positive Affirmations

I am _____

_____

_____

_____

_____

Date : ..../...................../...................   Feeling: 😐 😐 😐 😐 😊 − ——— +

Today, I am grateful for _____

_____

_____

_____

_____

Positive Affirmations

I am _____

_____

_____

_____

_____

❝
Favorite Quote
❞

Date : ..../...................../...................   Feeling: 😐 😐 😐 😐 😊 − ——— +

Today, I am grateful for _____

_____

_____

_____

_____

Positive Affirmations

I am _____

_____

_____

_____

_____

Date : ..../................../................

Feeling:

Today, I am grateful for _____

_____

_____

_____

_____

Positive Affirmations

I am _____

_____

_____

_____

_____

66   Favorite Quote   99

Date : ..../................../................

Feeling:

Today, I am grateful for _____

_____

_____

_____

_____

Positive Affirmations

I am _____

_____

_____

_____

_____

Date : ..../..................../....................   Feeling: 😣 😖 😐 😕 🙂

Today, I am grateful for _____

_____

_____

_____

_____

Positive Affirmations

I am _____

_____

_____

_____

_____

66 Favorite Quote **99**

Date : ..../..................../....................   Feeling: 😣 😖 😐 😕 🙂

Today, I am grateful for _____

_____

_____

_____

_____

Positive Affirmations

I am _____

_____

_____

_____

_____

Date : ..../............../...............   Feeling: 🙂 😐 😊 😊 😄

Today, I am grateful for _____

_____

_____

_____

_____

Positive Affirmations

I am _____

_____

_____

_____

_____

66   Favorite Quote   99

Date : ..../............../...............   Feeling: 🙂 😐 😊 😊 😄

Today, I am grateful for _____

_____

_____

_____

_____

Positive Affirmations

I am _____

_____

_____

_____

_____

Date : ..../..................../................   Feeling: 😊 😊 😊 😊 😊

Today, I am grateful for _____

_____

_____

_____

_____

Positive Affirmations

I am _____

_____

_____

_____

_____

66 Favorite Quote 99

Date : ..../..................../................   Feeling: 🙁 😐 😐 😊 😊

Today, I am grateful for _____

_____

_____

_____

_____

Positive Affirmations

I am _____

_____

_____

_____

_____

Date : ..../..................../...................   Feeling: 😡 😣 😐 😊 😄

Today, I am grateful for _____

_____

_____

_____

_____

Positive Affirmations

I am _____

_____

_____

_____

_____

❝   Favorite Quote   ❞

Date : ..../..................../...................   Feeling: 😡 😣 😐 😊 😄

Today, I am grateful for _____

_____

_____

_____

_____

Positive Affirmations

I am _____

_____

_____

_____

_____

"Why do you complain of your fate when you could so easily change it?"

— Marquis de Sade

Date : .... / .... / ....   Feeling: 😣 😐 😐 😊 😄
                                                        − ▬▬▬▬▬▬▬▬ +

Today, I am grateful for _____

_____

_____

_____

_____

Positive Affirmations

I am _____

_____

_____

_____

_____

❝   Favorite Quote   **❞**

Date : .... / .... / ....   Feeling: 😣 😐 😐 😐 😊
                                                        − ▬▬▬▬▬▬▬▬ +

Today, I am grateful for _____

_____

_____

_____

_____

Positive Affirmations

I am _____

_____

_____

_____

_____

Date : ..../................../................

Feeling:

Today, I am grateful for _____

_____

_____

_____

_____

Positive Affirmations

I am _____

_____

_____

_____

_____

66   Favorite Quote   99

Date : ..../................../................

Feeling:

Today, I am grateful for _____

_____

_____

_____

_____

Positive Affirmations

I am _____

_____

_____

_____

_____

Date : ..../................../................   Feeling: 😐 😐 😊 😊 😄

Today, I am grateful for _____

_____

_____

_____

_____

Positive Affirmations

I am _____

_____

_____

_____

_____

66   Favorite Quote   99

Date : ..../................../................   Feeling: 😐 😐 😐 😐 😄

Today, I am grateful for _____

_____

_____

_____

_____

Positive Affirmations

I am _____

_____

_____

_____

_____

Date : ..../.................../.................   Feeling: 😟 😕 😐 🙂 😄
                                                                         _ ▬▬▬▬▬▬ +

Today, I am grateful for _____

_____

_____

_____

_____

Positive Affirmations

I am _____

_____

_____

_____

_____

66   Favorite Quote   **99**

Date : ..../.................../.................   Feeling: 😟 😕 😐 🙂 😄
                                                                         _ ▬▬▬▬▬▬ +

Today, I am grateful for _____

_____

_____

_____

_____

Positive Affirmations

I am _____

_____

_____

_____

_____

Date : ..../................../................

Feeling: 😞 😐 😐 🙂 😊
_ ▬▬▬▬▬▬ +

Today, I am grateful for _____

_____

_____

_____

_____

Positive Affirmations

I am _____

_____

_____

_____

_____

66 Favorite Quote **99**

Date : ..../................../................

Feeling: 😞 😐 😐 🙂 😊
_ ▬▬▬▬▬▬ +

Today, I am grateful for _____

_____

_____

_____

_____

Positive Affirmations

I am _____

_____

_____

_____

_____

Date : ..../..................../...................   Feeling: 😠 😐 😐 🙂 😊 – ▭ +

Today, I am grateful for _____

_____

_____

_____

_____

Positive Affirmations

I am _____

_____

_____

_____

_____

66 Favorite Quote **99**

Date : ..../..................../...................   Feeling: 😠 😐 😐 🙂 😊 – ▭ +

Today, I am grateful for _____

_____

_____

_____

_____

Positive Affirmations

I am _____

_____

_____

_____

_____

Date : ..../..................../...................   Feeling: 😠 😐 😊 😄 😁 − ▬▬▬ +

Today, I am grateful for _____

_____

_____

_____

_____

Positive Affirmations

I am _____

_____

_____

_____

_____

66   Favorite Quote   99

Date : ..../..................../...................   Feeling: 😠 😐 😊 😄 😁 − ▬▬▬ +

Today, I am grateful for _____

_____

_____

_____

_____

Positive Affirmations

I am _____

_____

_____

_____

_____

Date : ..../................../................   Feeling: 😖 😣 😐 🙂 😄
                                                                              – ▬▬▬▬▬ +

Today, I am grateful for _____

_____

_____

_____

_____

Positive Affirmations

I am _____

_____

_____

_____

_____

❝   Favorite Quote   **❞**

Date : ..../................../................   Feeling: 😖 😣 😐 🙂 😄
                                                                              – ▬▬▬▬▬ +

Today, I am grateful for _____

_____

_____

_____

_____

Positive Affirmations

I am _____

_____

_____

_____

_____

Date : ..../..................../..................   Feeling: � 😐 😐 😊 😄
  − ▬▬▬▬▬ +

Today, I am grateful for _____

_____

_____

_____

_____

Positive Affirmations

I am _____

_____

_____

_____

_____

66 **Favorite Quote** 99

Date : ..../..................../..................   Feeling: 😊 😐 😐 😊 😄
  − ▬▬▬▬▬ +

Today, I am grateful for _____

_____

_____

_____

_____

Positive Affirmations

I am _____

_____

_____

_____

_____

Date : ..../.................../...................   Feeling: 😐 😐 😐 😐 😐

Today, I am grateful for _____

_____

_____

_____

_____

_____

Positive Affirmations

_I am_ _____

_____

_____

_____

_____

> ## Favorite Quote

Date : ..../.................../...................   Feeling: 😐 😐 😐 😐 😐

Today, I am grateful for _____

_____

_____

_____

_____

_____

Positive Affirmations

_I am_ _____

_____

_____

_____

_____

Date : ..../................./................

Feeling:

Today, I am grateful for _____

_____

_____

_____

_____

Positive Affirmations

I am _____

_____

_____

_____

_____

66   Favorite Quote   99

Date : ..../................./................

Feeling:

Today, I am grateful for _____

_____

_____

_____

_____

Positive Affirmations

I am _____

_____

_____

_____

_____

Date : ..../................../..................   Feeling: 😊 😊 😊 😊 😊
                                                     − +

Today, I am grateful for _____

_____

_____

_____

_____

Positive Affirmations

I am _____

_____

_____

_____

_____

> ❝   Favorite Quote   ❞

Date : ..../................../..................   Feeling: 😟 😟 😟 😊 😊
                                                     − +

Today, I am grateful for _____

_____

_____

_____

_____

Positive Affirmations

I am _____

_____

_____

_____

_____

Date : ..../.............../................   Feeling: 😊 😐 😐 😊 😊
                                                            – ~~~~~~~~~~~~~ +

Today, I am grateful for _____

_____

_____

_____

_____

Positive Affirmations

I am _____

_____

_____

_____

_____

❝   Favorite Quote   **❞**

Date : ..../.............../................   Feeling: 😞 😐 😐 😐 😊
                                                            – ~~~~~~~~~~~~~ +

Today, I am grateful for _____

_____

_____

_____

_____

Positive Affirmations

I am _____

_____

_____

_____

_____

Date : ..../............../................   Feeling: 😟 😐 🙂 😊 😄

Today, I am grateful for _____

_____

_____

_____

_____

Positive Affirmations

I am _____

_____

_____

_____

_____

66   Favorite Quote   **99**

Date : ..../............../................   Feeling: 😟 😐 😐 🙂 😄

Today, I am grateful for _____

_____

_____

_____

_____

Positive Affirmations

I am _____

_____

_____

_____

_____

Date : ..../................./................   Feeling: 😠 😦 😐 🙂 😄
                                                                    – ▬▬▬▬▬ +

Today, I am grateful for _____

_____

_____

_____

_____

                        Positive Affirmations
I am _____

_____

_____

_____

_____

66   Favorite Quote   **99**

Date : ..../................./................   Feeling: 😠 😦 😐 🙂 😄
                                                                    – ▬▬▬▬▬ +

Today, I am grateful for _____

_____

_____

_____

_____

                        Positive Affirmations
I am _____

_____

_____

_____

_____

"In all
things
of nature,
there is
something of
the marvelous."

— Aristotle

Date : ..../................../................

Feeling:

Today, I am grateful for _____

_____

_____

_____

_____

Positive Affirmations

I am _____

_____

_____

_____

_____

66 Favorite Quote **99**

Date : ..../................../................

Feeling:

Today, I am grateful for _____

_____

_____

_____

_____

Positive Affirmations

I am _____

_____

_____

_____

_____

Date : ..../.................../.................   Feeling: 😊 😐 😊 😊 😊
                                                                         − ——————— +

Today, I am grateful for _____

_____

_____

_____

_____

                           Positive Affirmations
I am _____

_____

_____

_____

_____

66   Favorite Quote   **99**

Date : ..../.................../.................   Feeling: 😊 😐 😐 😊 😊
                                                                         − ——————— +

Today, I am grateful for _____

_____

_____

_____

_____

                           Positive Affirmations
I am _____

_____

_____

_____

_____

Date : ..../................./................   Feeling: 😐 😕 😐 😊 😄

Today, I am grateful for _____

_____

_____

_____

_____

Positive Affirmations

I am _____

_____

_____

_____

_____

66   Favorite Quote   99

Date : ..../................./................   Feeling: 😐 😕 😐 😊 😄

Today, I am grateful for _____

_____

_____

_____

_____

Positive Affirmations

I am _____

_____

_____

_____

_____

Date : ..../................../................

Feeling:

Today, I am grateful for _____

_____

_____

_____

_____

Positive Affirmations

I am _____

_____

_____

_____

_____

66   Favorite Quote   99

Date : ..../................../................

Feeling:

Today, I am grateful for _____

_____

_____

_____

_____

Positive Affirmations

I am _____

_____

_____

_____

_____

Date : ..../................../..................   Feeling: 😐😐😐😐😐 − ══════ +

Today, I am grateful for _____

_____

_____

_____

_____

Positive Affirmations

I am _____

_____

_____

_____

_____

66   Favorite Quote   99

Date : ..../................../..................   Feeling: 😐😐😐😐😐 − ══════ →

Today, I am grateful for _____

_____

_____

_____

_____

Positive Affirmations

I am _____

_____

_____

_____

_____

Date : ..../.................../.................   Feeling: 😊😊😊😊😊

Today, I am grateful for _____

_____

_____

_____

_____

Positive Affirmations

I am _____

_____

_____

_____

_____

66   Favorite Quote   **99**

Date : ..../.................../.................   Feeling: 😣😣😐😊😊

Today, I am grateful for _____

_____

_____

_____

_____

Positive Affirmations

I am _____

_____

_____

_____

_____

Date : ..../..................../.................   Feeling: 😐 😕 😐 😊 😄
                                                                                      −   +

Today, I am grateful for _____

_____

_____

_____

_____

                              Positive Affirmations
I am _____

_____

_____

_____

_____

❝   Favorite Quote   ❞

Date : ..../..................../.................   Feeling: 😐 😕 😐 😊 😄
                                                                                      −   +

Today, I am grateful for _____

_____

_____

_____

_____

                              Positive Affirmations
I am _____

_____

_____

_____

_____

Date : ..../..................../....................   Feeling: 😀 😀 😀 😀 😀

Today, I am grateful for _____

_____

_____

_____

_____

Positive Affirmations

I am _____

_____

_____

_____

_____

❝   Favorite Quote   ❞

Date : ..../..................../....................   Feeling: 😀 😀 😀 😀 😀

Today, I am grateful for _____

_____

_____

_____

_____

Positive Affirmations

I am _____

_____

_____

_____

_____

Date : ..../..................../..................   Feeling: 😟 😧 😐 😊 😄

Today, I am grateful for _____

_____

_____

_____

_____

Positive Affirmations

I am _____

_____

_____

_____

_____

66   Favorite Quote   **99**

Date : ..../..................../..................   Feeling: 😟 😧 😐 😊 😄

Today, I am grateful for _____

_____

_____

_____

_____

Positive Affirmations

I am _____

_____

_____

_____

_____

Date : ..../..................../....................   Feeling:

Today, I am grateful for _____

_____

_____

_____

_____

Positive Affirmations

I am _____

_____

_____

_____

_____

66   Favorite Quote   99

Date : ..../..................../....................   Feeling:

Today, I am grateful for _____

_____

_____

_____

Positive Affirmations

I am _____

_____

_____

_____

Date : ..../........../............ Feeling: 😣 😖 😐 😊 😄
– ≈≈≈≈≈≈≈≈≈ +

Today, I am grateful for _____

_____

_____

_____

_____

Positive Affirmations

I am _____

_____

_____

_____

_____

66   Favorite Quote   99

Date : ..../........../............ Feeling: 😣 😖 😐 😊 😄
– ≈≈≈≈≈≈≈≈≈ +

Today, I am grateful for _____

_____

_____

_____

_____

Positive Affirmations

I am _____

_____

_____

_____

_____

Date : ..../...................../...................

Feeling:

Today, I am grateful for _____

_____

_____

_____

_____

Positive Affirmations

I am _____

_____

_____

_____

_____

" Favorite Quote "

Date : ..../...................../...................

Feeling:

Today, I am grateful for _____

_____

_____

_____

_____

Positive Affirmations

I am _____

_____

_____

_____

_____

Date : ..../.............../................ Feeling:

Today, I am grateful for _____

_____

_____

_____

_____

Positive Affirmations

I am _____

_____

_____

_____

_____

66   Favorite Quote   99

Date : ..../.............../................ Feeling:

Today, I am grateful for _____

_____

_____

_____

_____

Positive Affirmations

I am _____

_____

_____

_____

_____

Date : ..../.................../.................

Feeling: 😣 😐 😐 😐 😊

Today, I am grateful for _____

_____

_____

_____

_____

Positive Affirmations

I am _____

_____

_____

_____

_____

66   Favorite Quote   99

Date : ..../.................../.................

Feeling: 😣 😐 😐 😐 😊

Today, I am grateful for _____

_____

_____

_____

_____

Positive Affirmations

I am _____

_____

_____

_____

_____

Date : ..../................./................

Feeling:

Today, I am grateful for _____

_____

_____

_____

_____

Positive Affirmations

I am _____

_____

_____

_____

_____

66 Favorite Quote 99

Date : ..../................./................

Feeling:

Today, I am grateful for _____

_____

_____

_____

_____

Positive Affirmations

I am _____

_____

_____

_____

_____

Affirmations Hint

✦ ⋆ ★ ⋆ ★ 🌙 ⋆ ★ ⋆ ✦

I am a beautiful, confident and successful person.

I am healthy, loveable and joyful in life.

I am passionate, creative and fun loving soul.

I am grateful to receive that job promotion.

I am glad to travel around the world and eat all my favorite cuisines.

I am thankful for all life is offering me with joy and success.

I love my beautiful body and healthy lifestyle.

I am worthy enough to live my dream life.

I enjoy everyday three warm meals and hot coffee with my loved ones.

I have the most beautiful, loving and supportive husband and kids.

I do what I want to do in life with people I love to work with.

I am successful in my business and it is thriving & growing everyday.

I am wealthy and successful in every aspect of life.

My health is improving everyday and I am enjoying it.

My work and business is generating huge income every month and I feel blessed.

My income and wealth is increasing day by day.

I am traveling to the destinations of my dream this year.

My family loves, adores and support me in every decision of my life.

I am in control of what all is happening in my life and I am ready to accept it.

How to Write Affirmations:
- Always write in the present tense.
- Always write in a positive sentence.
- Always write about yourself only as the main subject (I, me, and myself).
- Focus on what you want to have and receive and not what you don't want.
- Focus on receiving at its full potential, don't hold back your thoughts and words.
- Focus on how you want your life to be and live it today. Manifest it :)

For more books check out: **www.anasema.net**
Follow on Instagram: **@anasemapress**

Made in the USA
Las Vegas, NV
15 December 2024

d0676c41-7553-4519-8913-a7df20befbabR01

.